ZeNSPiRATiONS®

Inspirations

Designs to Feed Your Spirit

CREATE, COLOR, PATTERN, PLAY!

Joanne Fink

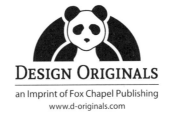

DESIGN ORIGINALS

an Imprint of Fox Chapel Publishing
www.d-originals.com

Basic Patterns

Patterning is fun, easy and relaxing—and it's a great way to add interest and texture to your designs. The nice thing about patterning is that patterns don't need to be perfect, just rhythmic. In fact, most patterns are more interesting when they have subtle variations. To practice patterning, start by drawing a series of horizontal lines. The lines don't need to be totally straight or evenly spaced. By drawing lines different distances apart, you'll create some narrower spaces and some wider spaces in which to pattern, as in the example below.

After drawing your lines, look at the step-by-step examples below. Pick the one you want to do and start by drawing step one of that pattern between two lines. The illustration below shows step one of the "Four Lines & a Circle" pattern.

Next, starting at the beginning of the line, draw step two on top of step one as shown below.

Then, draw step three on top of step two as shown below.

Repeat this process for as many steps as you choose. Patterning is cumulative; each step adds detail to the previous step, and each one can be used as a stand-alone pattern. If you want a simple pattern, stop after one or two steps; if you want a very detailed pattern, keep adding steps. The more steps you do, the more complicated and impressive your finished piece will look!

Filler Patterns

Patterning dates back to ancient times. Medieval manuscripts are replete with patterns comprised of lines, dots and other small fillers. Try some of these designs, or create your own filler patterns.

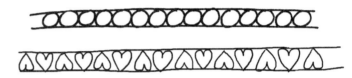

Triangle Pattern Variations

There are many ways to decorate a simple triangle pattern; here are some examples. I encourage you to experiment and try creating new patterns all your own.

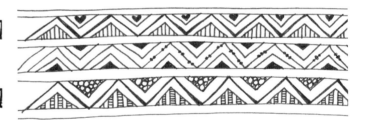

Patterns: Step by Step Examples

Four Lines & a Circle Pattern

step one | step two | step three | step four

Loop Pattern

Arch Pattern

step one | step two | step three | step four | step five | step six

Triangle Pattern

step one | step two | step three | step four | step five

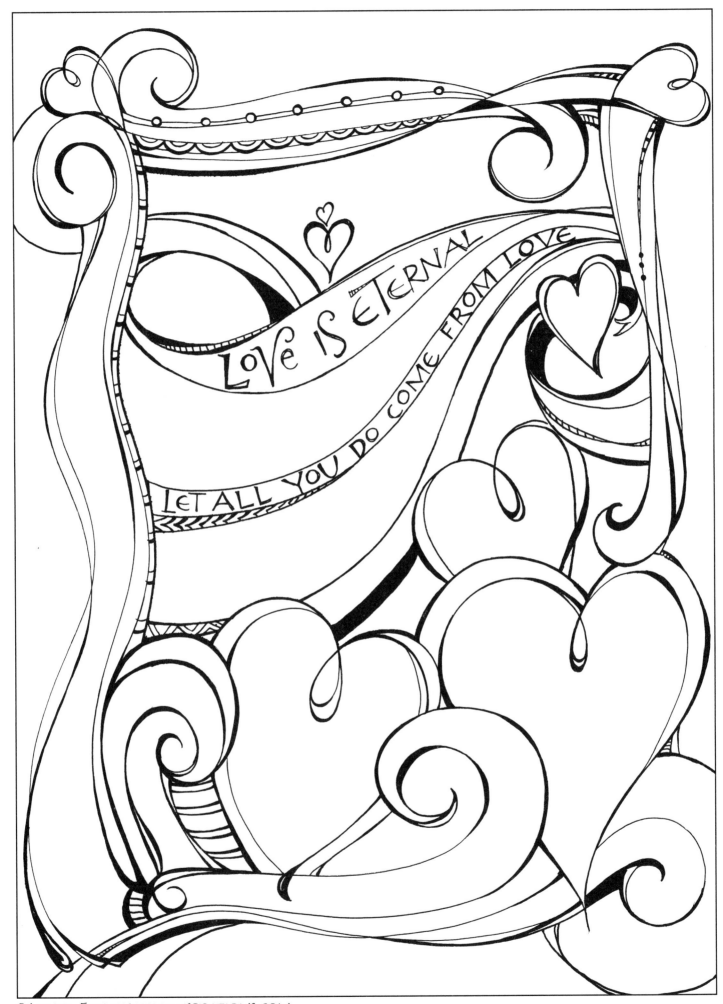

LOVE IS ETERNAL

LET ALL YOU DO COME FROM LOVE

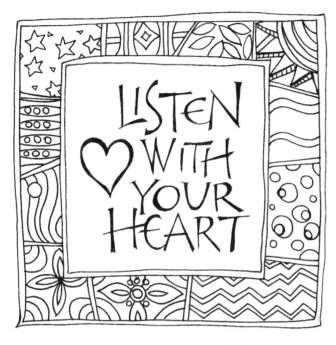

LISTEN WITH YOUR HEART

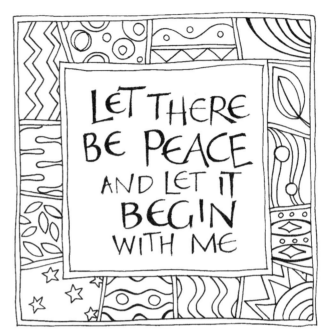

LET THERE BE PEACE AND LET IT BEGIN WITH ME

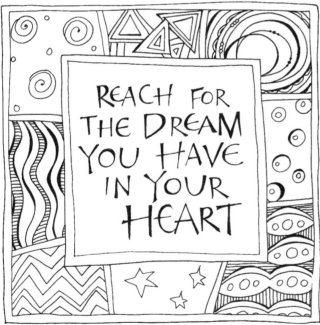

REACH FOR THE DREAM YOU HAVE IN YOUR HEART

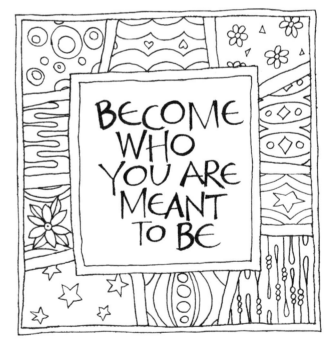

BECOME WHO YOU ARE MEANT TO BE

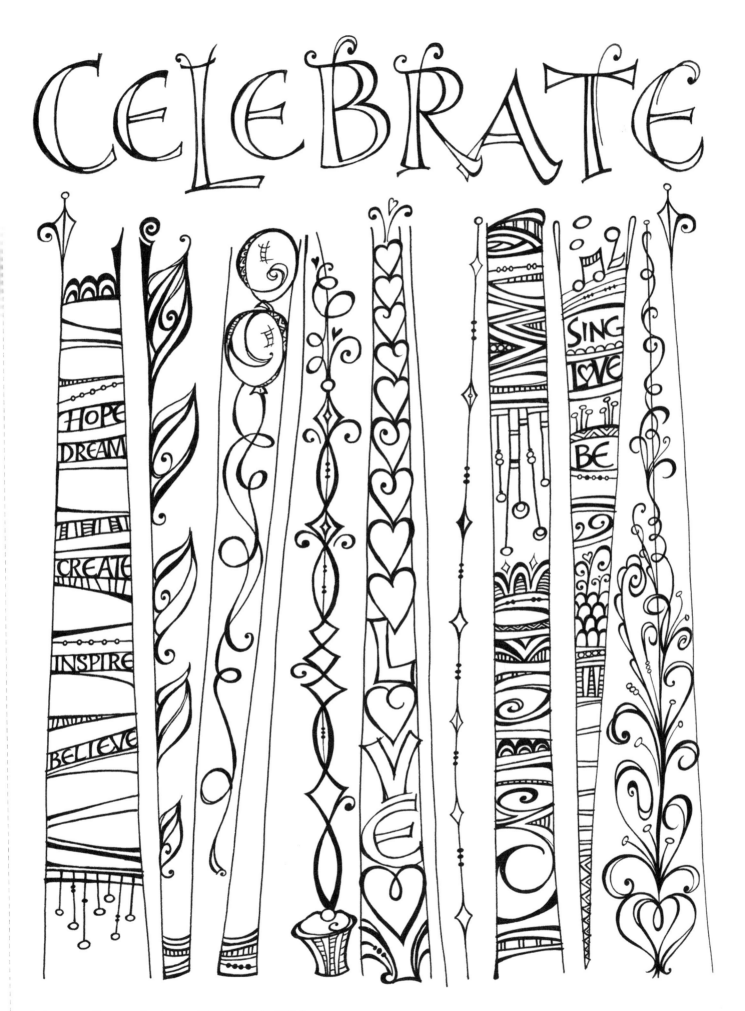

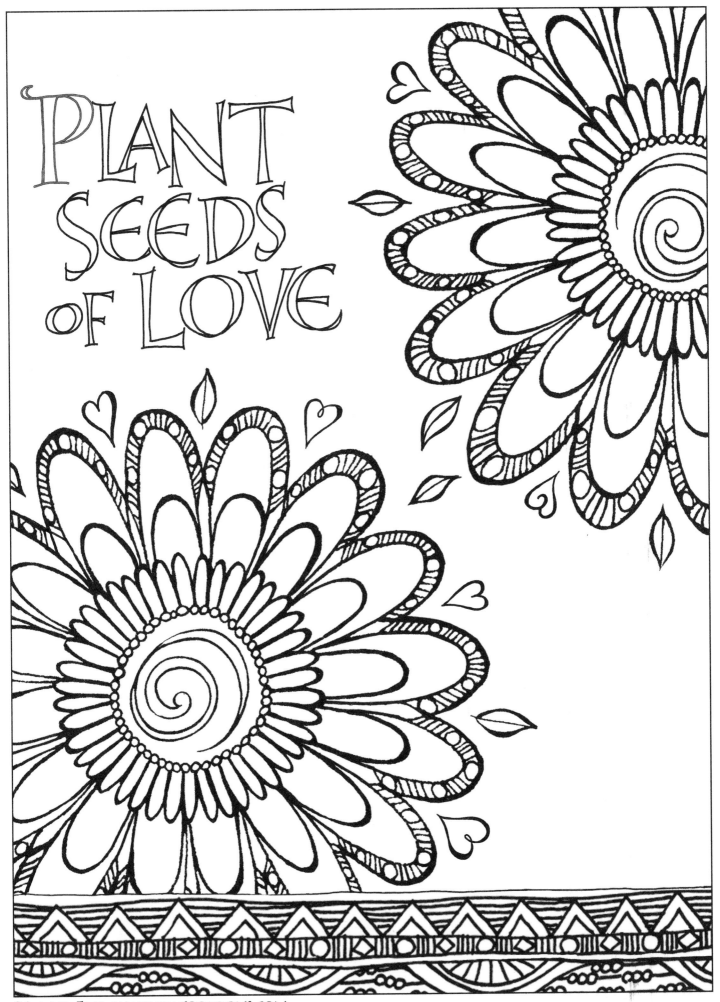

PLANT SEEDS OF LOVE

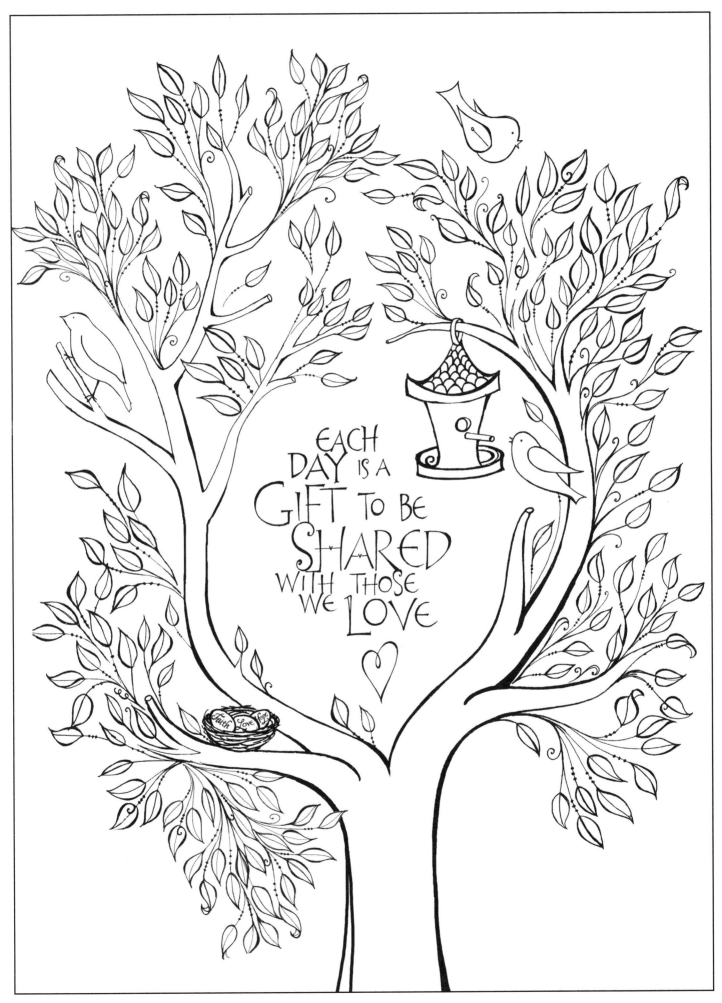

EACH DAY IS A GIFT TO BE SHARED WITH THOSE WE LOVE

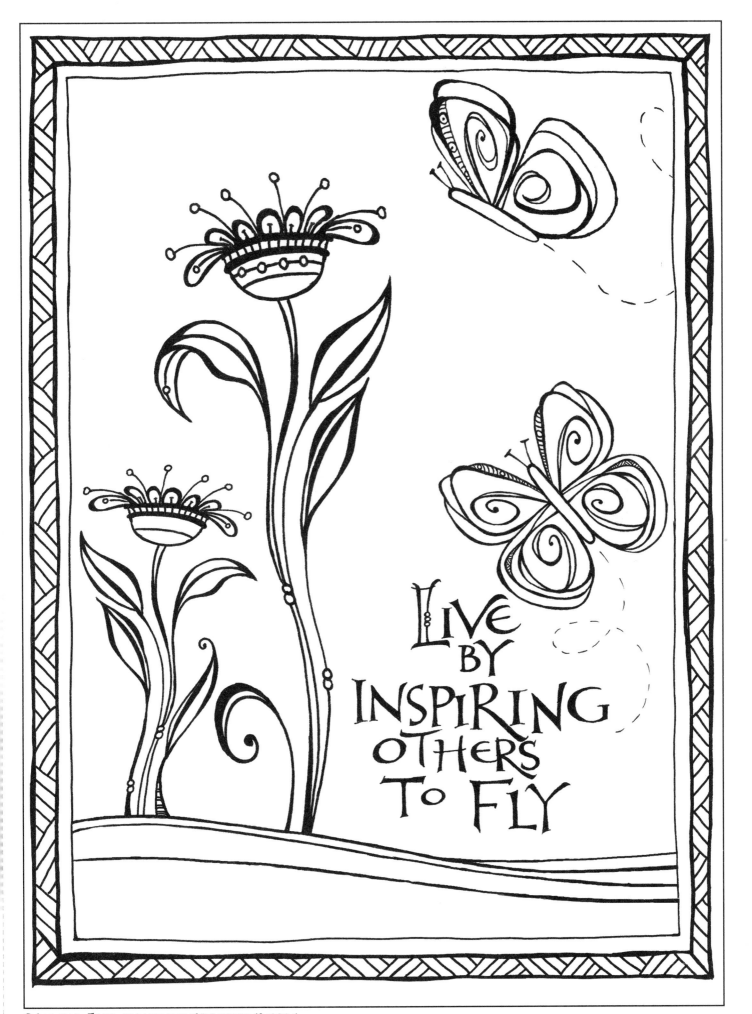

LIVE BY INSPIRING OTHERS TO FLY

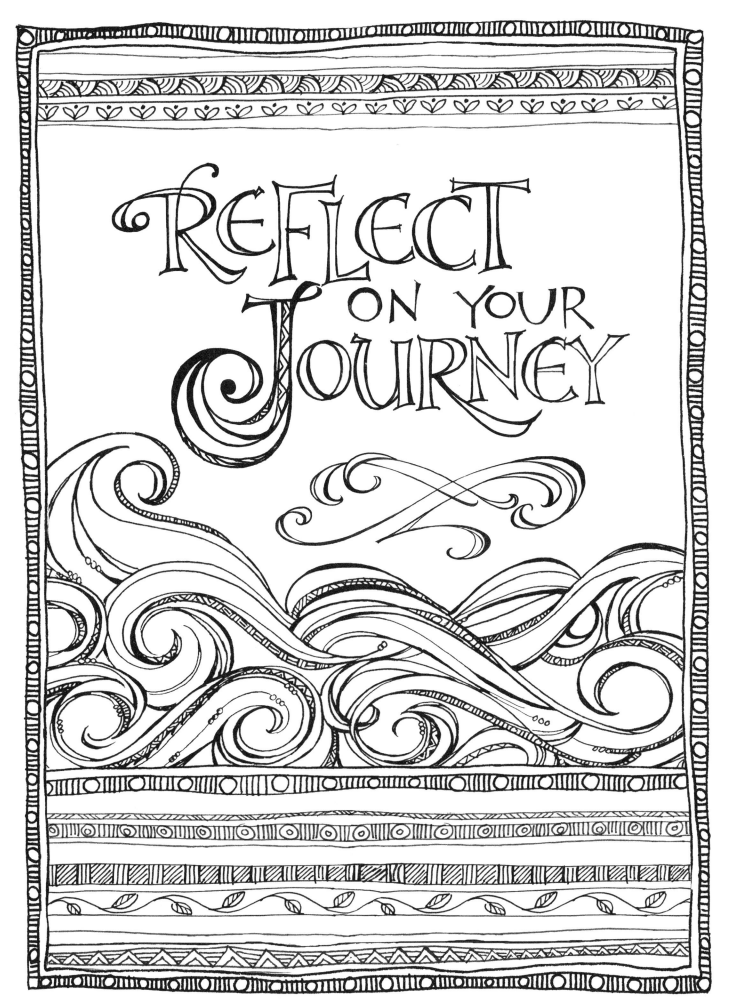

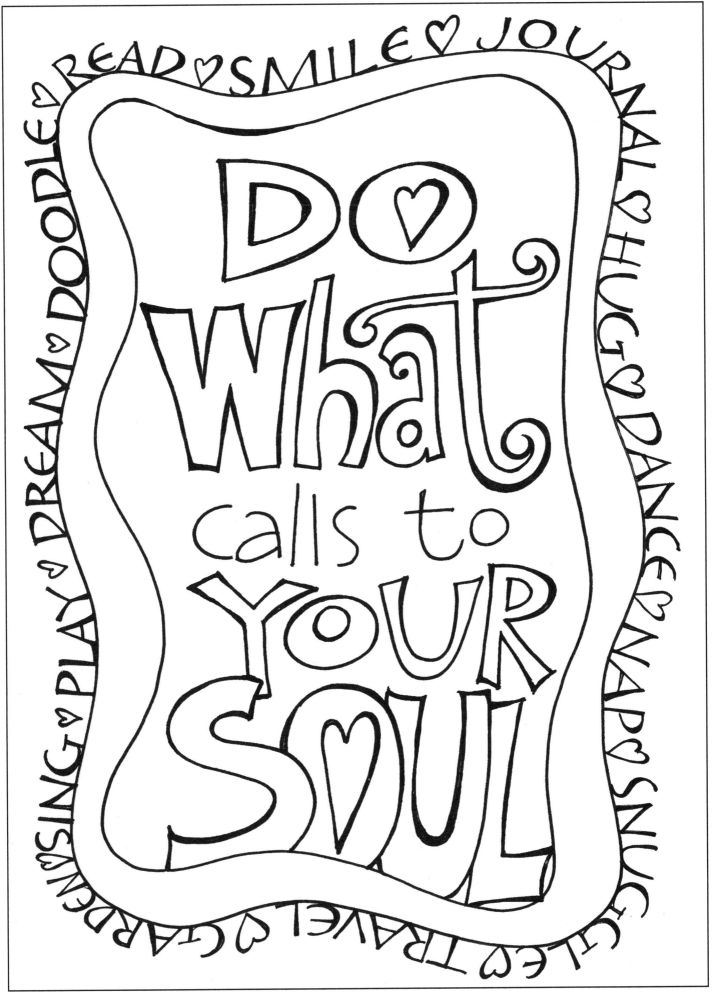

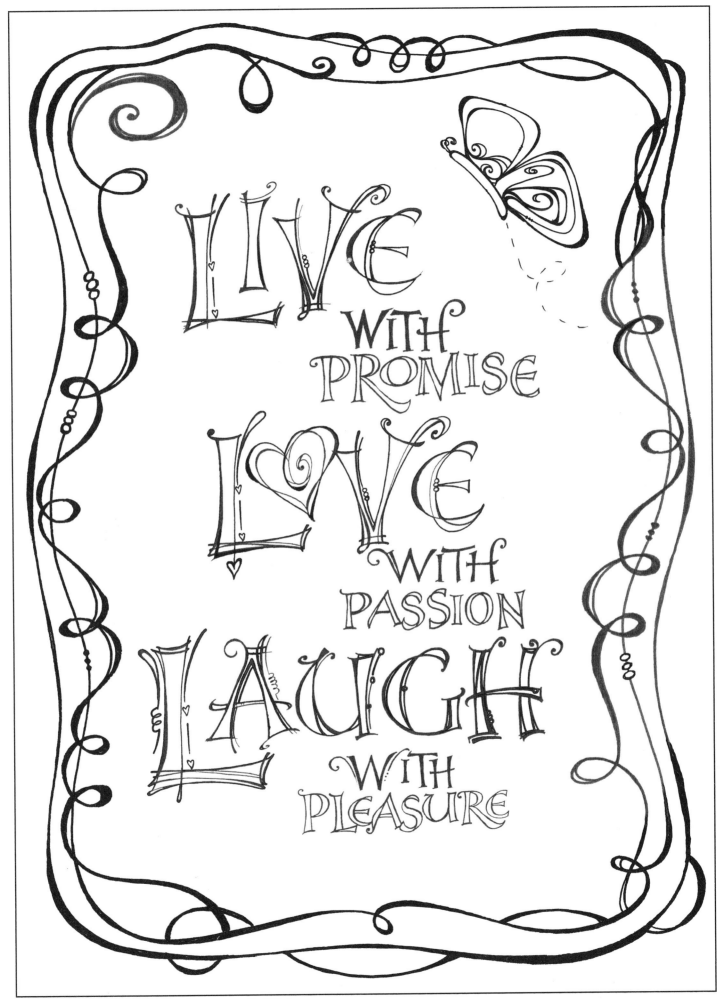

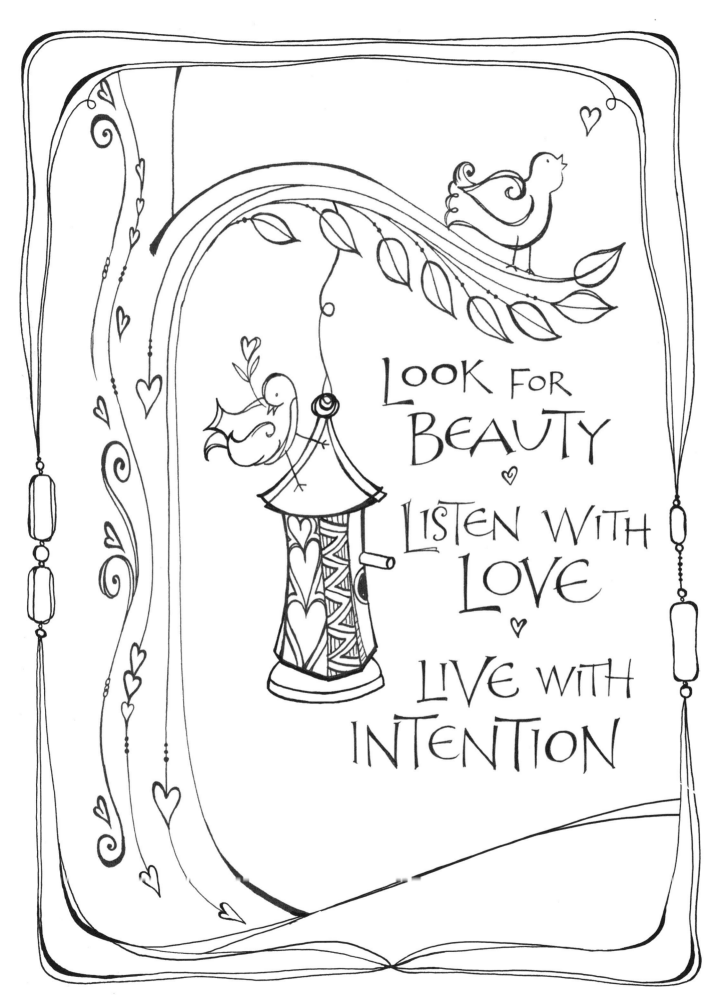

LOOK FOR BEAUTY

LISTEN WITH LOVE

LIVE WITH INTENTION

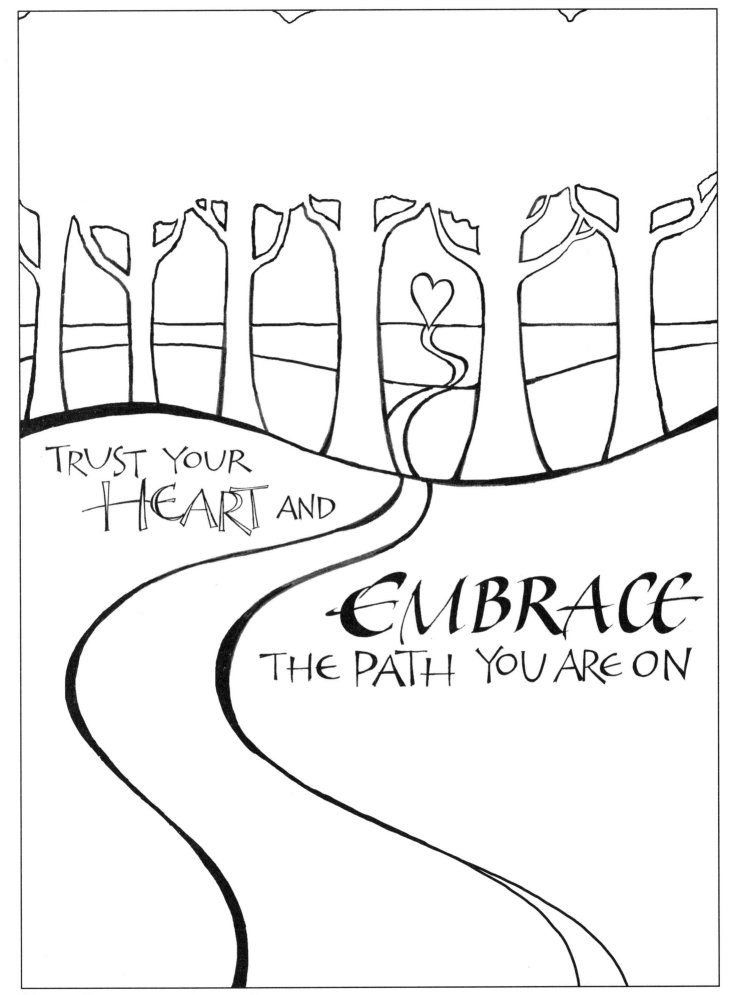

TRUST YOUR HEART AND EMBRACE THE PATH YOU ARE ON

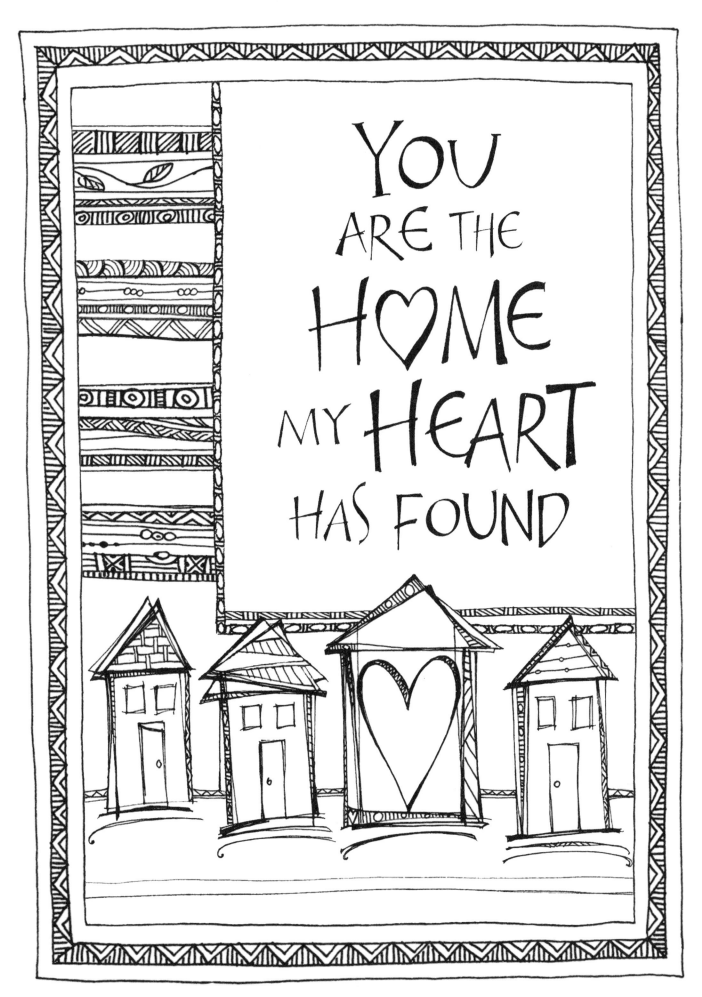

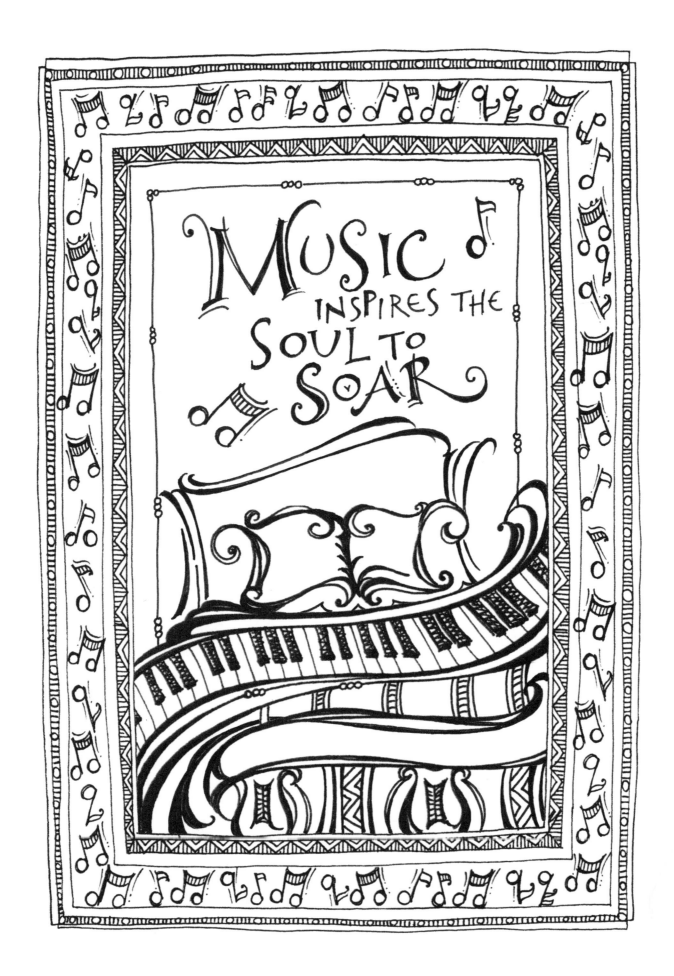

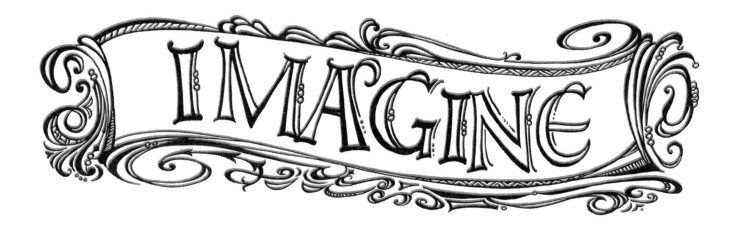

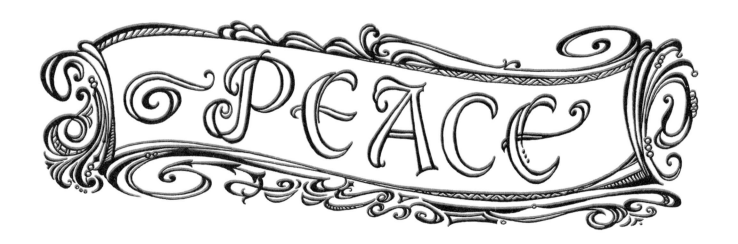

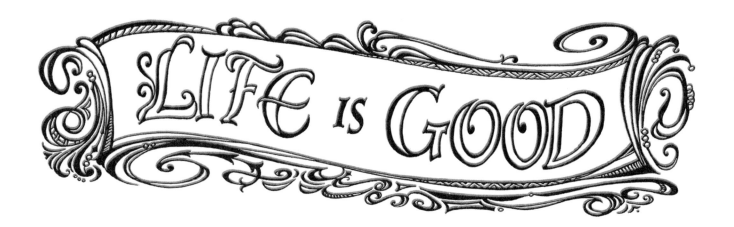

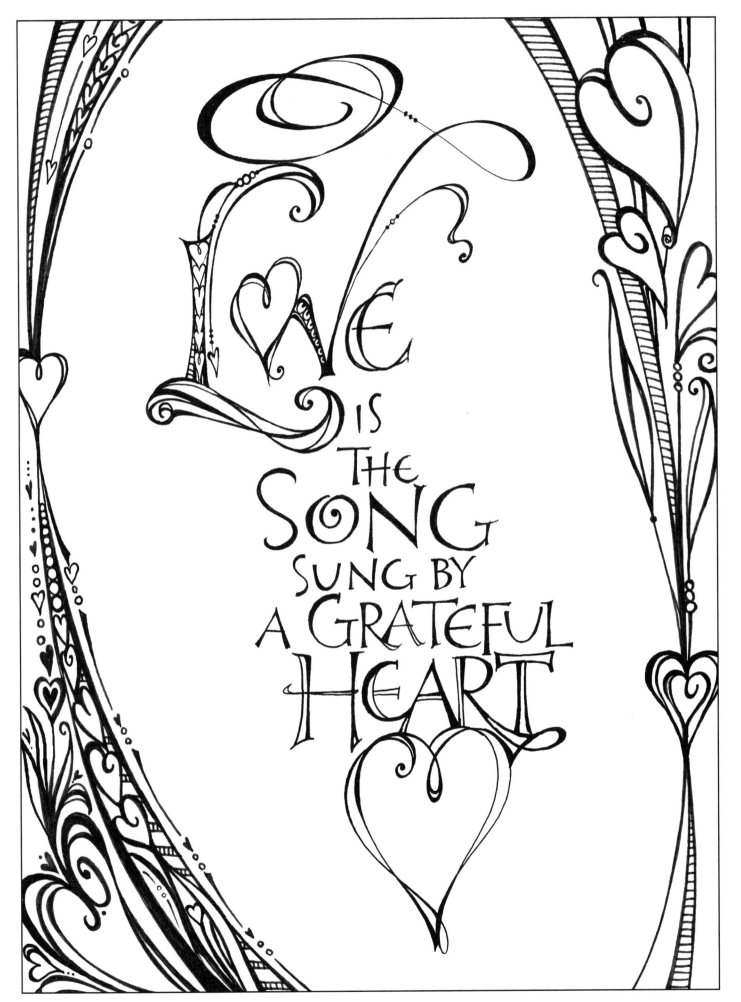

Love is the song sung by a grateful heart

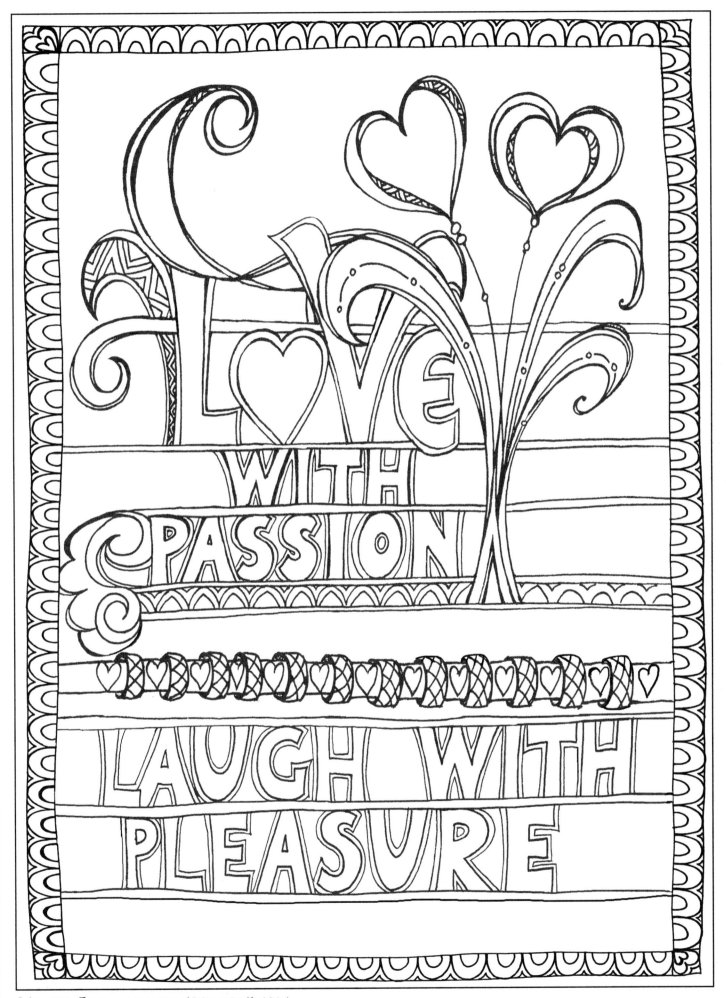

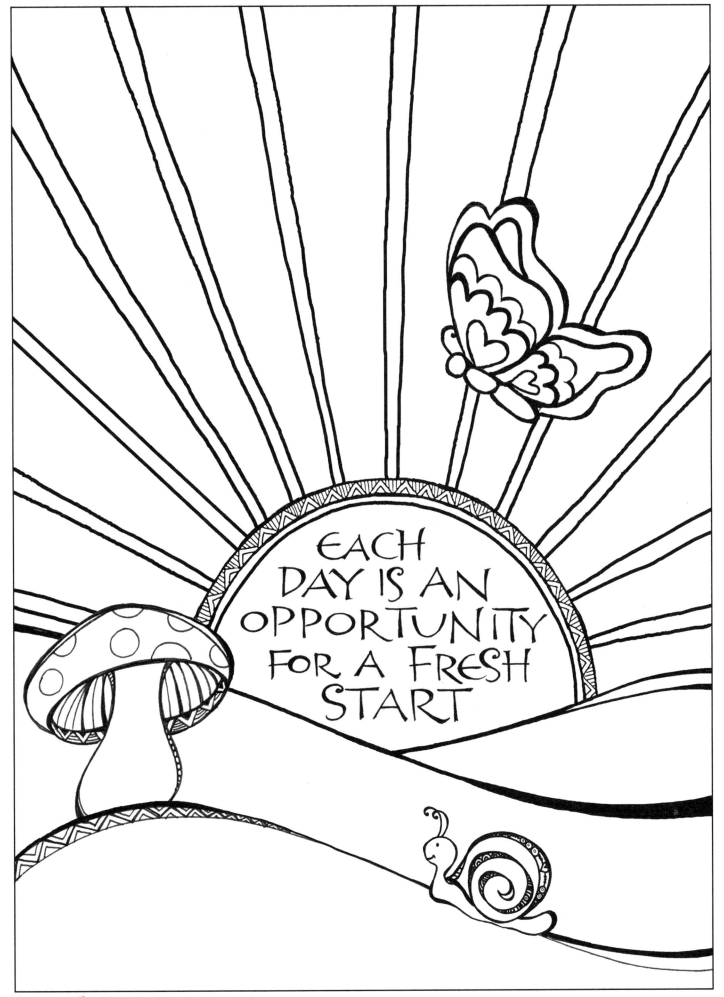

EACH DAY IS AN OPPORTUNITY FOR A FRESH START

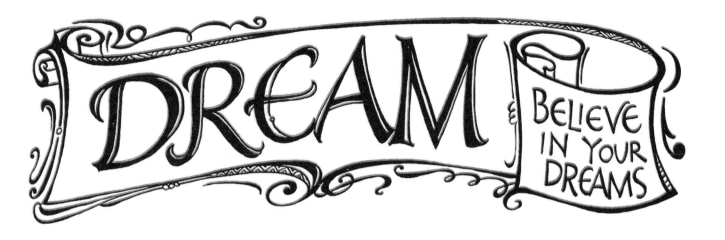

DREAM · BELIEVE IN YOUR DREAMS

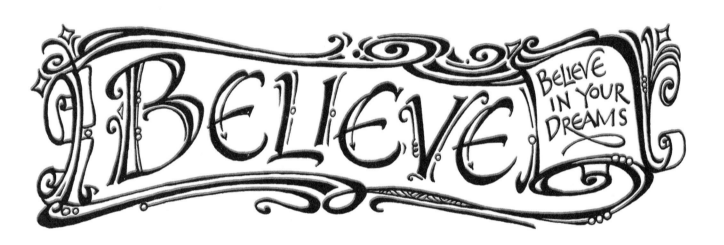

BELIEVE · BELIEVE IN YOUR DREAMS

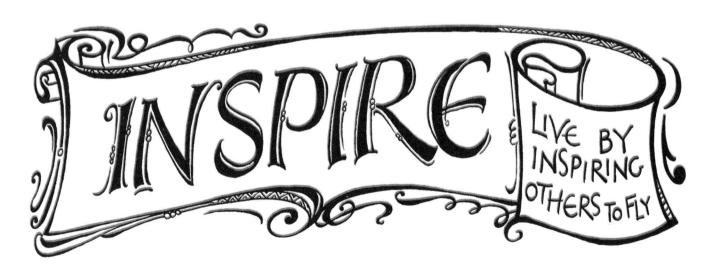

INSPIRE · LIVE BY INSPIRING OTHERS TO FLY

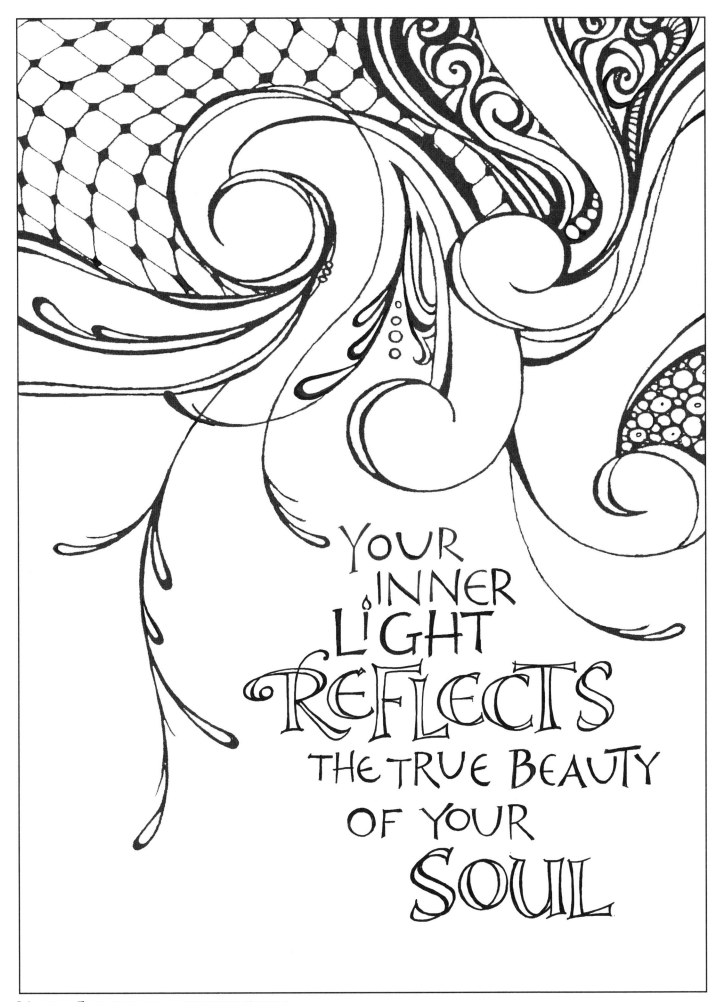

YOUR INNER LIGHT REFLECTS THE TRUE BEAUTY OF YOUR SOUL

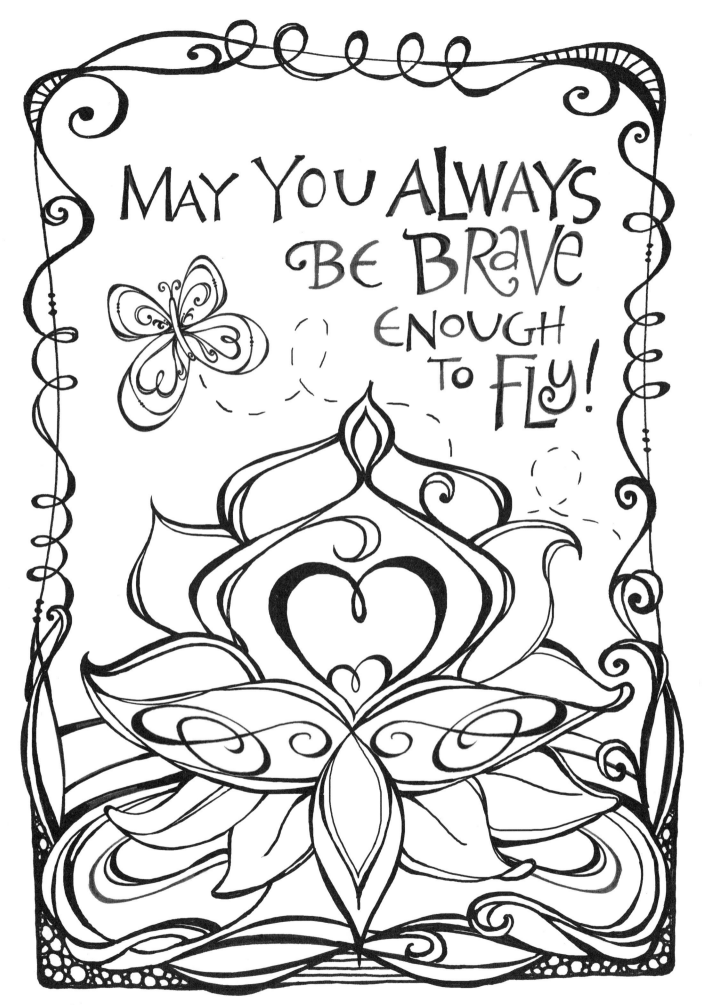

May You Always Be Brave enough to Fly!

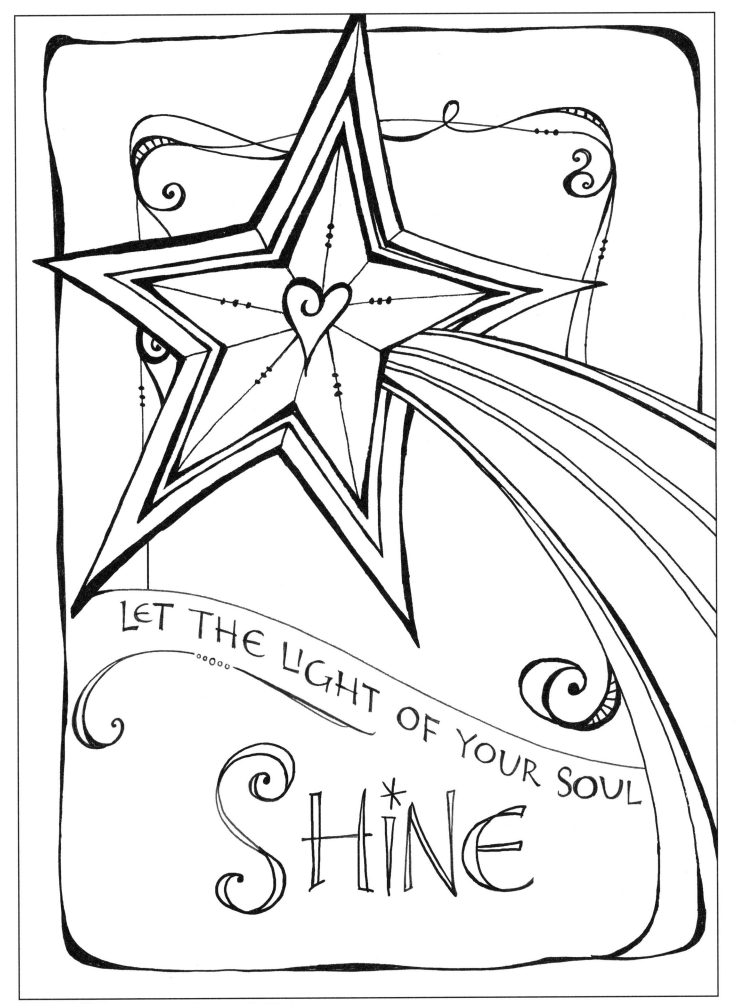

LET THE LIGHT OF YOUR SOUL SHINE

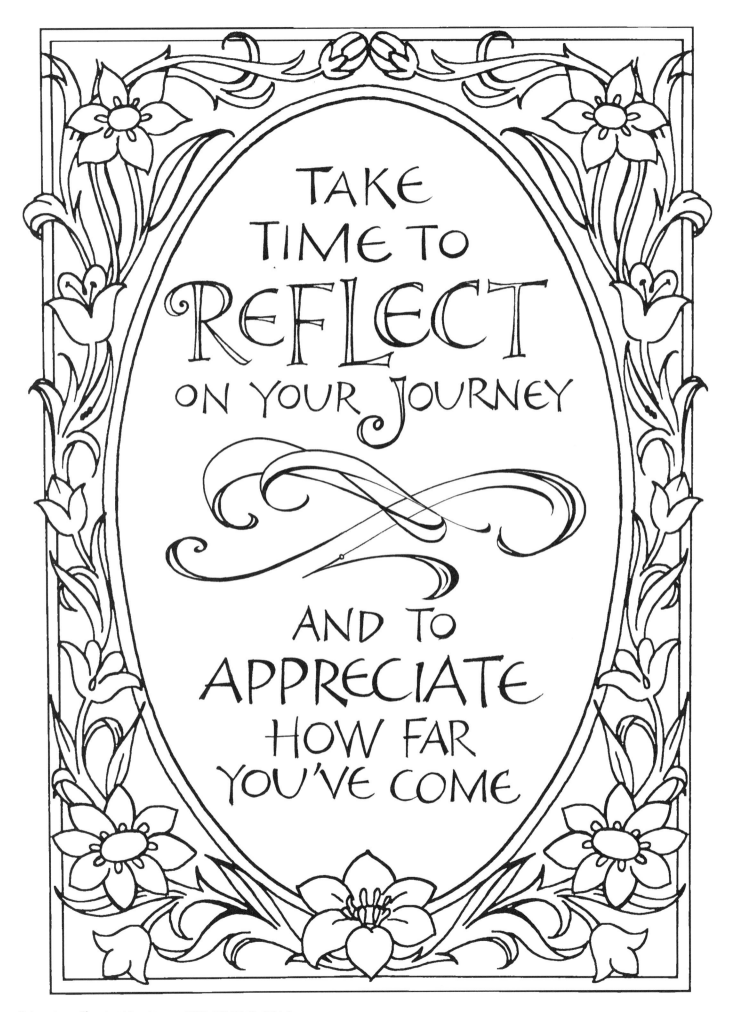

TAKE
TIME TO
REFLECT
ON YOUR JOURNEY

AND TO
APPRECIATE
HOW FAR
YOU'VE COME

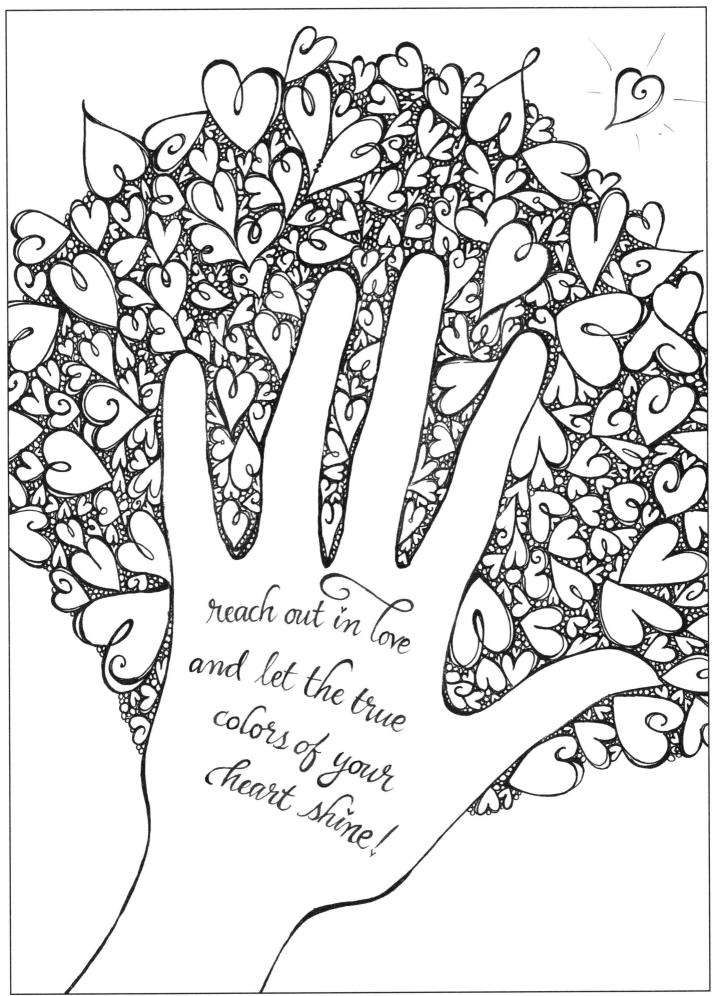

reach out in love and let the true colors of your heart shine!

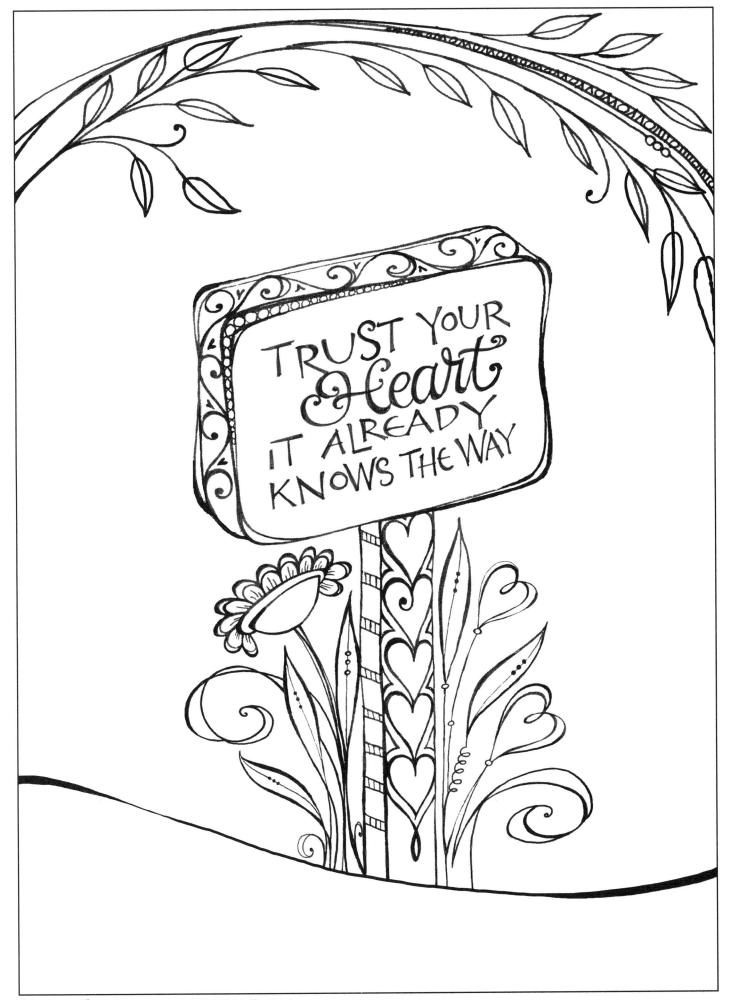

TRUST YOUR Heart IT ALREADY KNOWS THE WAY

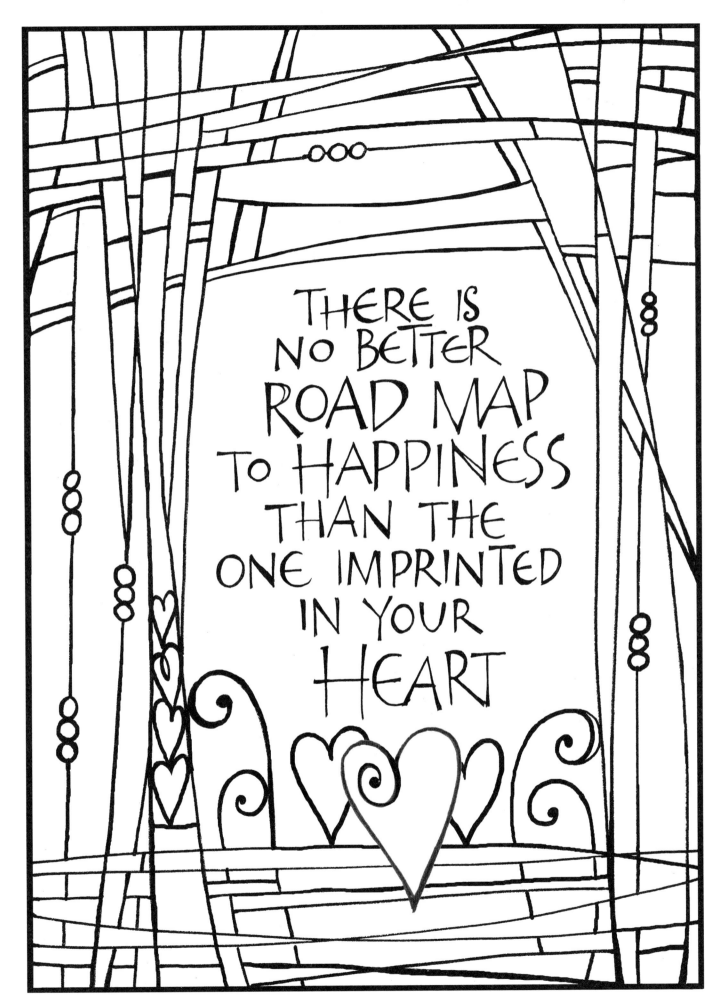

THERE IS NO BETTER ROAD MAP TO HAPPINESS THAN THE ONE IMPRINTED IN YOUR HEART

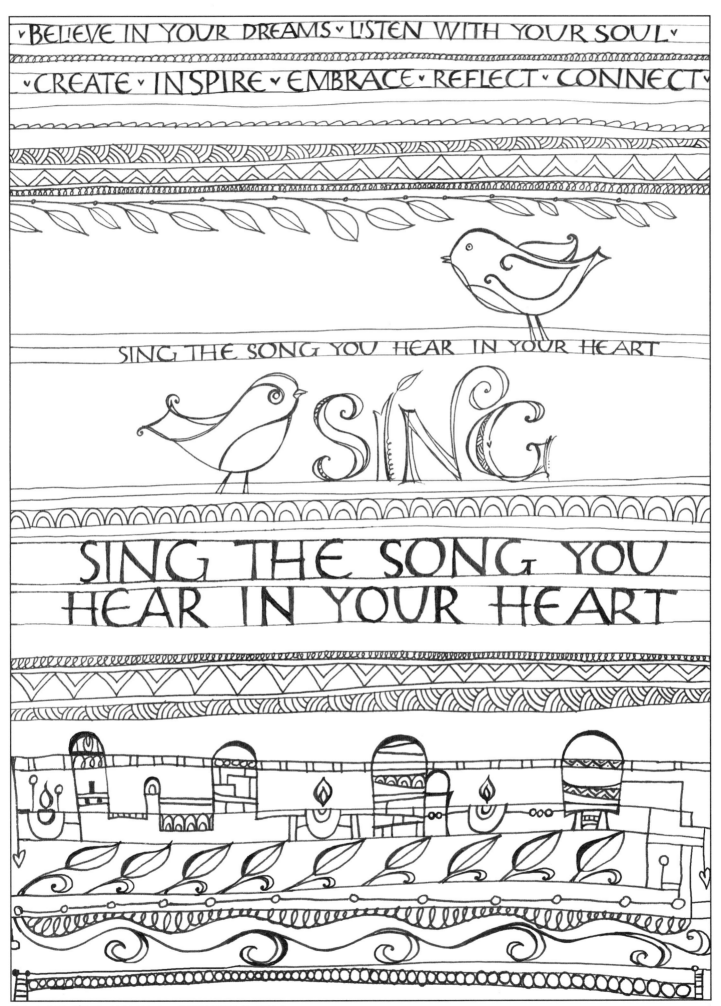

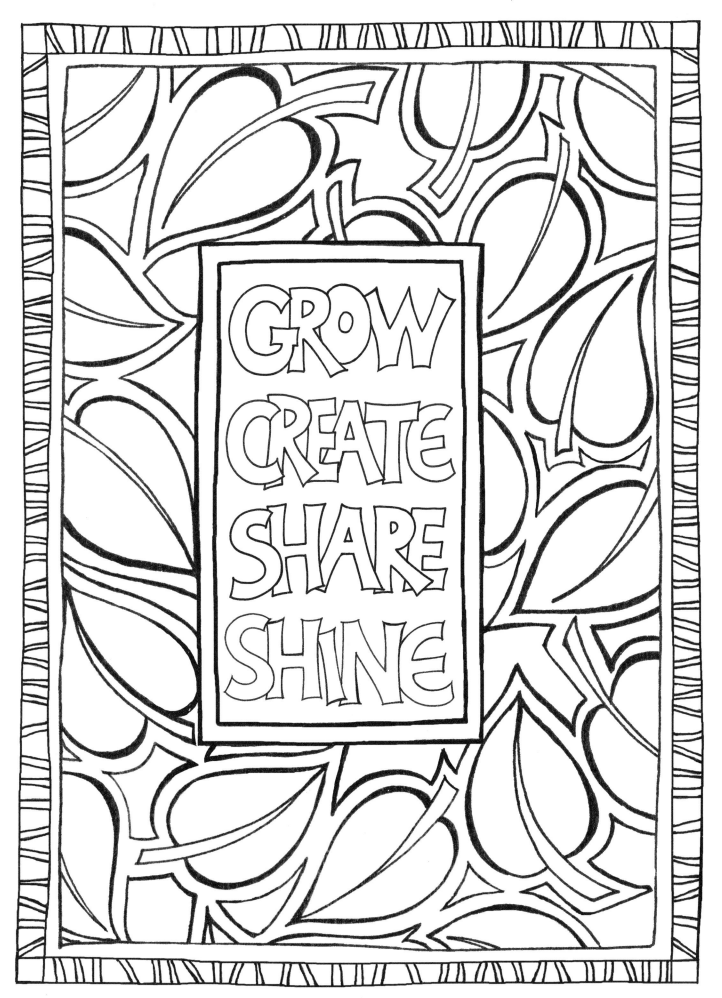

GROW CREATE SHARE SHINE